Adeyemo Aderonke

Export Made Easy

A Guide to Assist Beginners in Export Trade

BY

ADEYEMO ADERONKE

Copyright 2018 Aderonke Adeyemo
First Edition: May 2018

Published by:

STEM Business Academy

Tel: +234-1-8033774318

E-mail: stembusinessacademy@yahoo.com

Facebook Fan Page: http://bit.do/Stem-business-Academy

Address 25, Joseph Odunlami Street off Thomas Salako Street, Ogba. Lagos

No part of this book may be reproduced or transmitted, in any form or by any means, electronic or mechanical, including photocopy, recording or by any information storage or retrieval system without the express written permission of the author.

TABLE OF CONTENTS

EXPORT MADE EASY	1
COPYRIGHT 2018 ADERONKE ESTHER ADEYEMO	2
TABLE OF CONTENTS	4
ACKNOWLEDGMENT	6
INTRODUCTION	8
WHAT IS EXPORT	11
STEPS TO BE TAKEN TO BECOME AN EXPORTER	14
PLANNING FOR EXPORT	17
LIST OF EXPORTABLE PRODUCTS AND DESIGNATION TO BE MADE AVAILABLE (NIGERIA WESTERN ZONE)	20

ACTUAL EXPORTS COUNTRIES OF DESTINATION	31
MODE OF PAYMENT FOR EXPORT	38
EXPORT DOCUMENTATIONS	42
EXPORT DOCUMENTATION IN NIGERIA	45
NUGGETS ON EXPORT	56
DETAILED LIST OF EXPORTABLE PRODUCTS	67
SEMI PROCESSED/MANUFACTURED PRODUCTS	75
EXPORT FINANCING	109
OTHER BOOKS FROM THE SAME AUTHOR	115
ABOUT THE AUTHOR	116

ACKNOWLEDGMENT

My special thanks goes to the Almighty God, who is the father of light. He shines forth His light in my life and made me see what should be seen.

I say a special thank you to my family, husband and children.

My appreciation goes to Enterprise Development Centre of Pan Atlantic University for organizing a training on export.

Also, to the staff of Nigeria Export Promotion Council and finally the Federal Government of

Nigeria that decided to train few Nigerians on the business of Export Trade which I happened to benefit from (2013) 'New Exporters Development Program', I say a big thank you.

INTRODUCTION

As an evangelist that enjoys the grace of God in the area of soul winning, I thought my earthly assignment is to mainly win souls into the kingdom. However, I had an encounter with God seven years ago (2011) that changed my perspective.

The Lord asked me a question that shook me out of ignorance. He said "If Jesus was physically here in Nigeria, what do you think he will do about the economy of the nation".

He went further to remind how He had made me gained admission into Business Schools (even though they were on scholarship) to learn about entrepreneurship and later Export Trade.

He told me plainly that he wanted to equip me with certain knowledge so that I will be able to teach others.

He then said I should begin to run trainings/seminars on Export Trade so as to raise Exporters across the nation.

I was made to understand that we consume mostly imported things and refuse to export our own goods and services. 'Rise up and raise Exporters so that the nation economy becomes better'. That was the assignment I got from God.

I wrote this book in order to further answer the call of raising Exporters that will change the nation's economy, improve and contribute to GDP.

WHAT IS EXPORT

Export can be defined as selling abroad. Export is not done or completed until the seller has successfully gotten back his/her money. Products and services can be exported.

WHO IS AN EXPORTER

An exporter is someone or group of people selling abroad outside their home country.

TYPES OF EXPORTER

Manufacturing Exporter: They manufacture products and take their products abroad for sale outside of their country.

Export merchant: Export merchants buy products from manufactures and sell to buyers abroad,

Export Agent: An Export Agents finds a market and helps the manufacturer exports to the market. They acts as agents of the manufacturer.

TYPES OF EXPORT

Products and services

Products include

a. Agricultural commodities

b. Semi processed manufactured products

c. Processed manufactured products

d. Solid minerals

e. Arts and handicrafts

Services Include

(1) Engineering

(2) Medicals

(3) Entertainment

(4) Hair stylist

(5) Cultural Troupes

(6) Banking

(7) Fashion etc.

STEPS TO BE TAKEN TO BECOME AN EXPORTER

1. Possession of a registered limited liability company duly registered with the cooperate Affairs commission.

2. A Registered cooperative society with relevant agencies.

3. An NGO

For Registration with Nigeria Export promotion council. With originals of the following documents to be sighted schedule officer.

1. Limited Liability Companies.

a. Certificate of incorporation

b. Certified true copy of memorandum and articles of association.

c. Current certified true copy of form C07 (particulars of directors)

2. Cooperative Societies

   a. Certificate of Registration [issued by issuing Authority in the state and FCT].

   b. Bye laws of the society.

3 Government and Non government Organization

   a. Certificate of Registration

   b. Constitution of the NGO

c. Memorandum for guidance of applicant.

In additions to the above named documents, the following are also required:

- Cash payment of registration fee subject to review from time to time.

- Open a domiciliary account

- Identify a buyer overseas

PLANNING FOR EXPORT

You must be able to answer these questions:

a. Objectives: Why are you considering exporting?

b. Products: What do you want to offer the export market?

c. Promotion: How do you promote the product and service?

d. Strategy: How do you plan to enter the market?

These will make you to know if you are export ready or not.

Product Sourcing

§ Sufficient technical knowledge of the product in

question

- Identity product within your locality for export
- Location of where to source the product
- Product quality based on market specification
- Sufficient quantity to meet up with the order.

HINDRANCES IN EXPORT

1. Lack of adequate information
2. Lack of sufficient funding
3. Greed and get rich quick syndrome
4. High criminal tendencies / corruption
5. Non compliance with foreign standards

BENEFITS OF EXPORT

1. Foreign exchange generation Robust Economy

2. Promotion of made in Nigerian goods

3. Employment generation

4. Expansion of business

5. Diversification of sources of income and foreign exchange inflow.

LIST OF EXPORTABLE PRODUCTS AND DESIGNATION TO BE MADE AVAILABLE (NIGERIA WESTERN ZONE)

PRODUCTS	DESTINATIONS
Ginger	Germany, Holland, Finland
Chillies	Germany, Finland
Benniseed	Switzerland
Kenaf	U.K., USA
Sheanut	U.K., USA
Cotton Lint	Uk, Belgium, Sweden, Netherlands
Cotton Seed	Taiwan, Yugoslavia, Tunisia

Gum Arabic	Taiwan, Yugoslavia, Tunisia
Ceramic	USA, India
Alum	Sweden
Galvanized Pipe	Ecowas Market
Industrial Wires & Ropes	Ecowas Market
P.V.C. Pipe and Fittings	Dubai
Paper & Paper Products	
Bitumen	Cote D'Ivoire
Bicycles	Mali
Building Materials	Sweden
Towel and Napkins	Ecowas Market
Electrical Car Components	Senegal, Guinea
Blanket and Upholstery	Ghana, Namibia, Burkina

Faso

Dry Cell Batteries	Cameroun and Tchad
Furniture Cement Klinker	European Communities
Foam Products	Mali, Niger
Rug and Carpets	Ecowas Market, Korea
Plastic products & Tea	Ecowas Market
Cotton Yam	Europe and Bangladesh
Confectionaries	Europe, U.S.A
Insecticides	Niger, Cameroun, Tchad
Tropical Fruit Juices	Congo, Cameroun, Benin Republic
Leather & Leather Products	Sweden
Grinding Machines	Belgium, Holand

Tarpaulin products	Benin Republic, Niger, Tchad
Electric Metres & Circuits	Tunisia, Niger
Breaker	Mali
Insecticides	Ghana, Senegal, Cote D'Ivoire, Togo
Electronics	Mali, South Korea, Sweden
Furniture	Sweden
Nails & Wire Products	Togo, Burkina faso
Biscuits & Confectionery	Zaire, Congo
Vegetable Oil	Germany, U.K.
Animals Feeds	Niger, Tchad
Ceramic Tiles & Tubs	Sweden, Ecowas Market
Burnt Bricks	Ecowas Market
Iron & Steel products	Japan, Ghana
Handcraft &	

Calabash Carving	U.K., U.S.A.
Raffia Mats	Burkina Faso, Cote D'Ivoire
Soap & Detergents	U.S.A, Pakistan
Cotton Yam	U.K., Niger
Cement	Niger, Tchad
Foam Products	Niger, Tchad
Towels & Bed Spread	Senegal, Ghana
Threads	Chad, Cameroun, Kenya
Storage Tanks	Ecowas Market
Aluminum & Products	Burkina Faso
Ointment & Cosmetics	Ecowas Market
Stationeries	Belgium
Building Materials	Malta, Cote D'Ivoire
Sugar Cane	Malta, Saudi Arabia
Onions	Germany, Italy, France, U.K
Tomatoes	Saudi Arabia, U.K., Kuwait,

Dubai	
Millet	Saudi Arabia, Poland
Mangoes	U.S.A., Germany, France
Henna Weed	Germany, France, U.K., Netherlands, U.S.A.
Wood Carvings	Thailand, Sweden, Germany, Pakistan
Kaolin	Belgium, Sweden, U.S.A.
Gem Stone	West Indies, U.S.A., Europe
Fruit Juice	Burkina Faso
Honey	Germany, Italy, France, U.K.
Cowpeas	U.S.A., Britain
Potatoes	
Groundnuts	Saudi Arabia
Sorghum	Germany, Italy
Locust Beans	Sweden

Red Soreel (Remes Acetoma)	Sweden, Saudi Arabia, Belgium
Tobacco Leaves	Germany, France, Italy, U.K., Belgium
Cashew Nuts	Netherlands
Soya Beans	Germany, France, Italy, U.K., Belgium
Silica	Netherlands
Potash	Germany, France, Italy, U.K., Belgium, Netherlands
Columbite	Germany, France, Italy, U.K., Belgium, Netherlands
Glass	Iran
Feldspar	Iran
Antomone	Poland, Italy, France, U.K., Belgium
Granite	Netherlands
Limestone	Poland, Italy, France, U.K.,

Belgium, Netherlands		
Gypsum	Poland, Italy, France, U.K., Belgium, Netherlands	
Phosphate	Poland, Italy, France, U.K., Belgium, Netherlands	
Gold	Poland, Italy, France, U.K., Belgium, Netherlands	
Mica	Iran	
Beads	U.S.A.	
Cassava	Sweden, U.S.A., Kenya, Germany	
Yams	Sweden, U.K.	
Sweet Potatoes	Sweden	

Soya Beans Oil	Jeddah
Marble	Belgium, India
Carrot	Niger, Saudi Arabia
Lettuce	Saudi Arabia
Cow Horns	U.S.A., Europe
Diamond	Germany, Italy, U.K., U.S.A.
Quartz	Germany, Italy, U.K., U.S.A.
Leather	Poland, Sweden, Korea, Netherlands, India
Cigarette	U.S.A.
Beer	
Textiles	U.S.A., Netherlands, Equitorial Guinea, Czechoslovakia
Automobiles Accessories	Equitorial Guinea

ACTUAL EXPORTS COUNTRIES OF DESTINATION

PRODUCTS DESTINATION

A. **COMMODITIES**

Bones	U.K., Japan
Cassava	U.K.
Cashew Nuts	Hong Kong, U.K., India
Charcoal	Italy, Indonesia
Chillies	U.S.A, U.K.
Cocoa, Beans	Switzerland, France, U.K., Holland, U.S.A, Belgium

Coffee	Netherlands, Singapore
Cotton Leaf	Belgium, U.S.A
Fish	U.K.
Fruits	Switzerland
Ginger	Europe
Groundnut Seed	Belgium, U.S.A
Gum Arabic	Russia
Horns (Cow)	U.K.
Horns tips (Cow)	Japan
Colanut	Japan, France
Rubber	France, Cedex
Sesame Seed	Singapore, Spain, U.K., U.S.A
Sheanuts	Belgium, U.K.

Shrimps	U.K.
Skins	U.S.A, Channel Island, Spain, Belgium
Snails	Italy, Russia
Tobacco	U.K.
Vegetable	Belgium
Wheat Pellets	Europe
Yam	Puerto Rico, U.K.

B. MINERAL PRODUCTS

Columbite Ore	Belgium, U.K
Kaolin	Taiwan
Marble Stone	Taiwan

Tin Metal Ingot	U.K.
Zinc Alloy Ingot	Taiwan

C. MANUFACTURED/SEMI-MANUFACTURED PRODUCTS

Alkylate	Germany
Aluminium J-Bolts with nuts	Ghana
Auto Components	Ghana
Baby Clothes and Other Baby Products	Ghana, Cote D'Ivore, Guinea
Bic Points and Stoppers	Ghana
Bottle (Empty)	The Gambia, Ghana, Cote D'Ivoire
Calcium Carbonate	Ghana
Camel Back Cushion Repair Gum	Ghana
Chemicals	Senegal, Ghana, France

Carbon Black	Republic of South Africa
Cocoa Butter	Netherlands, U.K., Holland\
Cocoa Cake	U.K., Holland
Cocoa Powder	Holland
Cosmetics and Soaps	U.S.A, Ghana
Cotton, Yam	Spain, U.K., Belgium
Cylinders	Germany
Delvac 1340	Togo, Ghana, Cote D'Ivoire
Detergents	Ghana
Doors (Wooden)	U.K.
Drilling Equipments	United Arab Emirate
Filament	U.K.
Floor Parquets	U.K.
Furniture Components	U.K., Baizers, Vaduz, Belgium
Glass Sheets	U.K.
Glycerin	Ghana, Cameroun, Zaire, Russia
Groundnut Seeds	U.K.

Groundnut Oil	Taiwan
Hoof Powder	Ghana, Togo, Cote D'Ivoire, Senegal
Insecticides	Senegal, Liberia, Cote D'Ivoire
Jars (Empty)	Cote D'Ivoire, Ghana, Togo Benin Republic
Lubricants	U.K.
Malt Drink	Ghana
Milo (Bulk)	U.K., Belgium, Holland
Palm Kernel Cake	U.K., Belgium
Palm Kernel Oil	Congo, Brazzaville
Peugeots Cars	Ghana
Pharmaceutical Products	The Gambia
Plastic Wares (Including Crates)	Spain, Belgium
Polyester Yam	U.S.A
Polyester Chip	The Gambia, Guinea, Cote D'Ivoire

Pound Yam	Ghana
Printed Cotton	Ghana
Printing Ink	Cote D'Ivoire
Retreading Materials	Ghana, Cote D'Ivoire
Botex/Powder Container	U.K.
Royco (Spices)	U.K.
Scrap Copper Wire	U.K.
Scrap Metal	Italy, Switzerland
Slicing Veneer	U.K., Thailand, The Gambia, Guinea
Swashes	U.K.
Textiles	U.S.A.
T-Shirts	Ghana
Tomapep	Ghana
Tyres and Tubes	U.K.
Tiles and Adhesives	
Venus Salon Cloth	

HANDICRAFTS

Assorted Handicrafts	U.S.A

MODE OF PAYMENT FOR EXPORT

One of the most critical aspects of trade is getting paid. International trading partners can conduct business never having even met.

It is therefore very important to consider how an exporter expects to be paid which must be in agreement with the buyer.

Different Methods of Payment

Cash in advance:- Buyer pays for the goods before the seller ships.

Open Account:- Seller ships first and buyer pays later

Documentary Collection:- Seller is able to collect payment from an oversea buyer through intermediary bank.

Letters of Credit:- A written undertaking of a bank on behalf of its customer to pay a specific amount in the agreed currency provided the beneficiary submit documents within the prescribed deadlines.

The Consignment Method:- The seller ships the goods to the buyer, broker or distributor, but will not receive payment until the goods are sold or transferred to another buyer. This is mostly applicable to fresh or perishable goods. The money will be paid to the exporter only after the sales of the goods.

Credit Card:- Some banks offer special lines of

credit that are accessible in a credit card to facilitate substantial purchases.

Countertrade and Barter:- This is most often used when the buyer lacks access to convertible currency or finds that rates are unfavourable or can exchange for products or services desirable to the seller. The buyer will compensate the seller in a manner other than transfer of money. Barter is the exchange of goods or services between two parties.

Getting paid can be affected by

Problems with the country

Problems with the customer

Problems with the goods

Problems with the shipment

Adeyemo Aderonke

Problems with the finance

Problems with the documents

All can be protected against with the knowledge of a good administration, good communication, good international trade knowledge.

EXPORT DOCUMENTATIONS

Documentation is more important than the goods. Documents are required to prove that all functions have been affected.

Export documents are needed for

Logistics reasons

Payment reasons

Legal reasons

Financial reasons

Political reasons

Ecological reasons

Or a combination of these, traders needs to know

How to complete them

How to check them

Where to get them

Where to send them

Why they are required

Documents must be

Accurate

Contain enough information

Fit for the purpose

Produced quickly

Neat

The most common export documents

Quotations

Order confirmations

Invoices

Packing lists

Certificates of origin. – C16 combined

Certificate of value and origin.

EXPORT DOCUMENTATION IN NIGERIA

S/NO	TITLE OF DOCUMENT	USE(S) OF DOCUMENT	WHERE OBTAINABLE
1.	Exporters Registration Certificate	To obtain database of Exporters and as a precondition for the export of Non-oil Export in Nigeria	Nigerian Export Promotion Council (NEPC)
2.	Nigeria Export	An	Commercia

	Proceeds Form (NXP FORM)	evidence of intent to export formally with details of the transaction.	l Banks.
3.	Commercial Invoice	Provides details of Transaction and indicate financial obligations.	Exporter
4.	Certificate of Origin	To certify that the	Nigerian Association

			product(s) originate(s) (manufactured & produced) from Nigeria	Of Chambers Of Commerce, Industry Mines & Agricultural (NACCIMA)
5.		Clean Certificate Of Inspection (CCI)	Independent statutory report on the Product specification, quality	Cobalt International Services Limited

			and value.	
6.		Certificate Of Sampling, Weight, Quality And Loading	(Optional) For Product quality certification	SGS Or Any Other Inspection Company
7.		Phytosanitary Certificate	Conditions for both exporting and importing countries to ensure safety in the	Nigeria Agricultural Quarantine Services (Fed. Min. of Agriculture & Natural Resource.

		handling of Agricultural product and natural resources free from diseases	
8.	Packing List	A list of Product exported with units, quantity, sizes & shapes.	The Export Agent/Exporter
9.	Bill of	A	Shipping

	Leading/Airway bill/Way bill	document acknowledging the receipt of goods for sea, air and land travel. It has the date of export and mode of transport.	Company/ Airline/Land Transports
10.	Certificate of Marine Insurance	(Optional) To cover the	Insurance Company.

			liability of Goods in transit defined for export.	
11.		Certificate of Quality Fumigation And Weight	Evidence of fumigation especially for Agricultural Products and their weight (evidence of	Federal Produce Inspection Service, (Federal Ministry of Trade & Investment)

		quality).	
12.	Product Quality Certification	Ensuring Product Standards for both local & Export, especially manufactured Products.	Standards Organization Of Nigeria (SON)
13.	Single Goods Declaration (SGD)	Provides the particulars of inspected export consignment ready	Nigeria Customs Services.

			for shipment.	
14.	Form ICO-1		Term for the payment of Agricultural commodity levies as stipulated bylaw.	Federal Ministry of Trade & Investment
15.	Certificate of clearance form		For export of handicrafts and artifacts.	Department of National Museum & Monument

16.	Certificate of quality for food and drugs	To certify the quality of Drugs, Food and Cosmetics meant for export	NAFDAC
17.	Form J	Clearance letter for the export of solid minerals	Fed Ministry of Solid Minerals
18.	Clearance from the Dept. of Forestry	For exports classified endanger	Department of Forestry

		ed wild life species, wood and wood products, furniture and furniture components.	
19.	Aquatic Resource Permit	For Exports of fishery and aquatic products	Federal Department of Fisheries
20.	Article/memorandum of	For registrati	Corporate Affairs

	Association	on with NEPC	Commission
21.	Certificate of Analysis	To certify the quality of the product in question	Issued by Manufacturers, processors of Mines.
22.	Certificate of clearance from National Museums and Monuments	For export of handicrafts and art crafts	National Commission for Museums and Monuments
23.	Certificate of Commodity export	Issued for payment	Federal Ministry of Industry

			of exported levy on agricultural commodities being exported from Nigeria	Trade and Investment
24.		Certificate of Incorporation	For legal identity and registration with NEPC and other relevant agencies	CAC

25.	Certificate of Conformance	To show that standardized quality has been achieved and maintained	SON
26.	Health Certificate	Certifies the quality of foods, drug and cosmetics meant for exports.	NAFDAC
27.	Certificate of	For	Issuing

	Registration	registration as a cooperative with NEPC	Authority in the State and FCT
28.	Certified Invoice	Needed for independent Verification	Chamber of Commerce
29.	Export License from Department of Forestry	For export of classified endangered wild life species, Wood	Federal Department of Forestry, Federal Ministry of Environment

			products, Furniture and furniture components	
30.		Consular Invoice	Enables Invoice to be validated or checked by importing country's Consulate	Consulate of country of destination
31.		ETLS Certificate	Allows	NEPC,

			duty free trade for goods amongst ECOWAS member country under the ECOWAS TRADE Liberalizations scheme	MoFA ECOWAS
32.		Exporter permit/Certificate of clearance from Veterinary Health Services	For export of animal and animal products	Department of Livestock services, FMARD

33.	Exporter Registration Certificate	For identification of Nigeria exporter	NEPC
34.	Final/Commercial Invoice	Accounting document prepared in the name of the importer or his agent to take care of charges	Exporter

			and enable customs in the importing country assess duty payable	
35.	CAC 1 (Availability Check and reservation of name)		For registration with CAC	CAC
36.	CAC 2 (Statement of share capital and return allotment)		For registration with CAC	CAC

37.	CAC 2.1 (Particulars of Company Secretary)	For registration with CAC	CAC
38.	CAC 3 (Notice of situation or change of registered address)	For registration with CAC	CAC
39.	From Co7 (Particulars of Director)	For registration with CAC	CAC
40.	GSP Form	For tariff concession for all countries involved in North-	NACCIMA, NCS

		south trade	
41.	ICCO-1 Certificate	Combined certificate of origin and declaration of value of cocoa levy	Federal Ministry of Industry, Trade and Investment, Produce inspection Unit
42.	Insurance Certificate	Show evidence of insurance for the shipment	Insurance company

			and under CIF contract, is paid for by the exporter	
43.		MANCAP certificate MANCAP form MANCAP report	For Manufactures only	SON-MANCAP
44.		NIMASA From C series	For allocation of cargoes to shipping lines. It serves	NIMASA and Commercial Banks

		as cargo tracer and loading authorization to allotters	
45.	Non Commercial Exports (NCX) Form	For non-commercial exports	CBN and Commercial Banks
46.	NPX Form	For non-commercial exports originating from Nigeria	CBN and Commercial Banks

47.	Products Analysis Certificate	Requirement for SON-MANCAP registration	SON
48.	Pro-forma Invoice	A form of quotation by the exporter and often times required by the importing country for the purpose of foreign	Exporter

		exchange allocation	
49.	Single Goods Declaration (SGD) Form C2C10	Gives the particulars of consignment	NCS
50.	Import permit	For plants	NAQS

NUGGETS ON EXPORT

The Nigerian Export Promotion Council (NEPC) is Nigeria's local point for the development and promotion of export trade. Information on how to export and other assistance can be obtained from the office.

Export business involves a lot of documentation and procedures, so it is essential to acquire the necessary training. As a beginner, you need some basic knowledge as to how the export market works, documentation, port procedures, guidelines, product sourcing, pricing etc.

Define your products of interest and specify what products you can easily make available in required quantity and quality for export whenever there is demand for it.

Products can be sourced by buying from other sources to export or by producing yourself.

The products being exported haves to be of acceptable quality in the target market.

The products may have to be adapted in terms of quality, packaging and labeling in line with the dictate of the target market.

Packaging of your product has to be firm to be able to withstand the rigours of long distance transport, attractive to catch attention while on the shelve, environmentally friendly labels may sometimes need to be bilingual depending on the target market.

Mode of shipment will determine the type of packaging to use. Thus, packaging should take into consideration the customer's requirements, international standards, and regulations applicable in the target markets.

An Exporter needs to choose between exporting directly or through an intermediary. The choice of the distribution channels depends on the nature of the market, skills, finance etc.

Direct exporting involves advertising the product in the target market. Participation in international trade fairs and trade mission are helpful for accessing the market.

Do the due diligence check to ensure the credibility of prospective buyers

Avoid sharp practices in the business and be sincere in order to elicit trust and confidence of your buyer

Ensuring high quality product and services increases the chances for success in world market.

Branding gives product identity and enhances recognition. If a brand is well known, it wins consumer loyalty. Known brands are hard to displace in the marketplace.

The Nigerian Export Promotion Council (NEPC) conducts a number of trade promotion events that can assist exporters improve their business. They include trade missions, trade fairs and exhibitions, buyer-seller meetings, contact promotion programmes, and market surveys and investigations.

Trade shows and exhibitions provide appropriation forum for one-to-one interaction with consumers. Participating in these events gives you an opportunity to establish networks, enhance your brand and test market your products.

Information on products to export and target markets are available on NEPC product mapping at all NEPC offices. The Nigerian Export Promotion Council will provide guidance on export procedures for different export markets.

Like all other businesses, export marketing carries its own risks. Exporters should be aware of these risks and guard against them.

Because of distance barriers, an exporter may not understand fully the requirements of the target market.

Export trade benefits exporters in a number of ways. Business will be cushioned against fluctuations in local demand. You position yourself to utilize your excess capacity. You gain a share of global markets. Increase in sales and profits and contribute to the growth of the country's economy.

To know what markets to export to, consider how attractive they are in terms of demand, size and profits, purchasing power. Consider also the activities of competitors and whether they can be a problem to your entry.

Establish the potential of the market by undertaking some desk research to establish the size of the population, growth rate, market entry strategies and existing distribution channels.

If possible, visit the target market to verify your desk research and undertake assessment on the ground.

Also establish the existence of products similar to

yours, the value of their imports, imports tariffs, market requirements, per capita income, availability and cost of transport, and contacts in the target market.

Talk to potential importers and trade promotion organization in the target market.

Develop an export marketing plan.

You do not need to be a giant manufacturer to get into the export trade. All you need is a market, the right information and the right skills.

You will also need a product which can be adapted to meet the market standards and requirements, the right price to make your goods competitive in the export market and financial and human resources to develop your export business.

You also need a focused, dedicated and competent trade promotion organization to provide you with the necessary market information and marketing skills.

Proper packaging protects shapes and makes products attractive to consumers. You communicate with your consumer through packaging.

Timely delivery of your products is also a major plus.

Once you determine the markets you want to export to, you can access them through direct exporting, indirect exporting or through agents.

ETLS

ECOWAS Trade Liberalization Scheme (ETLS) is

the main tool for promoting West Africa as a free trade area. It permits the free movement of goods originating or produced in ECOWAS member-states by eliminating tariff and non-tariff barriers (customs duties, quotas, prohibitions or any such restrictions).

ETLS provide coverage for the following categories of products provided their origin is ECOWAS region: Agricultural goods, Livestock, Unprocessed goods, Artisan handicrafts and Industrial goods.

Agricultural goods and Artisan handicrafts do not require Certificate of Origin. They are to be traded duty free within the region but with the appropriate sanitary certificate from the Nigerian Agricultural Quarantine Services.

If an exporter wants to trade industrial goods duty

free within the region, he/she needs an ETLS Certificate of Origin to prove that the product originates from the ECOWAS region.

ETLS Certificate can be obtained from NEPC, Ministry of Foreign Affairs and ECOWAS Secretariat.

AGOA

The African Growth and Opportunity Act (AGOA) provide preferential market access to eligible sub-Saharan countries. 6,400 products are eligible.

NEPC runs an AGOA Centre in Lagos, which provides information and capacity development for exporters to access the US market through AGOA.

NEPC

The Nigerian Export Promotion Council (NEPC) provides advisory services to local exporters in such areas as export procedure and documentation, transportation, financing, marketing techniques, quality control, export packaging, costing and pricing, publicity and other similar activities.

NEPC pursues the simplification and streamlining of export procedures and documentation on continual basis.

NEPC conducts training courses for current and potential exporters to enable them acquire the knowledge and skills necessary for export trade.

DETAILED LIST OF EXPORTABLE PRODUCTS

AGRICULTURAL COMMODITIES

COCOA

Cocoa beans light crop

Cocoa beans main crop

TUBERS

Cassava & it's Derivatives

Cassava Chips

Cassava pellet

Cassava Flour

Cassava Starch

Cassava Glucose

Tapioca

Garri

Starch

Yams

Cocoyams

Potatoes

GUM ARABIC

Gum Arabic Grade 1

Gum Arabic Grade 2

Gum Arabic Grade 3

EDIBLE NUTS

Cashew nut (Raw)

Ground Nuts

Walnuts (in Shell)

NATURAL FIBERS

Cotton lint

Juice

Coconut fibers

SPICES

Chillies

Ginger (Dried, split)

Pepper

Cloves

CRUDE DRUG

Kola nuts (fresh & dried)

Bitter kola

HORTICULTURAL PRODUCTS

FRUITS

Avocadoes

Bananas

Guava

Lemons

Mangoes

Melon (Water)

Oranges

Pawpaw

Pine apples

Plantains

Tomatoes

VEGETABLES

Asparagus

Beans

Baby corn

Beetroot

Carrots

Cucumbers

Garlic

Lettuce

Mushrooms

Okra

Onions

Peas

Potatoes

Spinach

Red and white Sorrel (Harbicus Sabdariffa)

Dehydrated vegetable

Hibiscus Sorrel (Red & White)

CUT FLOWERS

Roses

MEDICINAL HEBS

Neem

Garlic

Lemon grass

Aloe Vera

OIL SEEDS

Coconut (Fresh)

Shea nuts

Shea butter

Coffee (Arabic/Robusta)

Sesame seed (Beni seed)

Egusi (Melon)

SEMI PROCESSED/MANUFACTURED PRODUCTS

SHRIMPS AND PRAWNS

Processed H. I. Brown

RUBBER CRUMPS

COW HORNS (Tips)

COCOA CAKE

COCOA BUTTER

COCOA POWDER

SHEA BUTTER

PALM KERNEL CAKE

ORANGE CONCENTRATES

PINEAPPLE JUICE CONCENTRATE

CASHEW KERNELS

GINGER POWDER

COTTON YARN

PROCESSED/MANUFACTURED PRODUCTS

COTTON PRODUCTS

Cotton thread

Cotton grey cloth

Textiles fabric

Cotton bags and sacks

Towels

Absorbent cotton wool

Cotton yam

TEXTILE PRODUCTS

Cotton super print African print

Cotton real wax

Cotton sheet

Bedspread and sheets

Mosquito nets

Table covers

Cushion covers

Linens and other furnishing articles

Napkins

Pillow cases

FINISHED LEATHER

(Goat, Sheep & Cow)

READY MADE GARMENTS

Adire batiks wears

Suits

Shirts

Safari Coats

Trousers

Customers and fashion

Children wears

Boubou

Beach wears

TEXTILE SECONDARY ACCESSORIES

Zippers

Fasteners

Buttons

CANVAS GOODS

Tents

Tarpaulins

Carpets and rugs

School bags

Canvas shoes

FOOTWEAR AND LEATHER PRODUCTS

Leather sandals

Leather slippers

Canvas shoes

Folders and bags

Shoes

Shoes soles

Belts

PETROLEUM AND PETROCHEMICAL PRODUCTS

Liquefied gas

Petroleum jelly

Bitumen

Steam Coal

Carbon Black

Polypropylene

Polythene Bags

Paraffin and wax

Aviation fuel

Motor spirit

Lubricants

Insecticide

CHEMICALS

Borax (anhydrate and decanhydrate)

Alcohol

Ammonium Nitrade

Acetic Acid

Benzene

Butadiene

Glycerine

Methanol

Photographic chemical

Magnesium carbonate

Hydrochloric acid

Hydrogen peroxide

Caustic soda

Phenol

Sulphuric acid

Toluene

Yeast

FERTILIZES

Urea

Nitro phosphate

Calcium ammonium Nitrate

Super phosphate

AUTOMOBILES

Peugeot brand of cars

Innoson brand of cars and utility Vehicles

AUTOMOTIVE PARTS

Brake pads and Linings

Batteries and casings

Auto cables

Mirrors

Tubes and Tyres

Rubber mats

Headlights and side lights

Fan belts

PAPER AND PAPER PRODUCTS

Poster papers

Print paper (Coated and impregnated)

Kraft liner in rolls or in sheet

Paper Board

Card Board

Paper for packing/packaging containers

Envelopes

Wall papers

Writing pads

Stationaries

IRON AND STEEL PRODUCTS

Machine tools and industrial parts

Wires and cables for telegram

Wires and cables for electrical installation

Galvanized pipes

Nails, screws, nuts etc

Corrugated iron sheets

Aluminum ingots

Zinc alloys

Iron & steels bars, rods etc

Gas cylinders and cookers

PLASTIC AND PLASTIC PRODUCTS

Plastic house wares, chairs, tables and house furniture

Pharmaceutical packaging

Shoe & slippers

Poly bags

Storage tanks and containers

PVC

VEGETABLE OILS/FATS AND CAKES

Cocoa butter

Cocoa cake

Coconut oil (crude/refined)

Fish oil (crude and refined)

Shea butter

Palm kernel oil (crude/refined)

Palm kernel cake

Sesame seed oil

Ginger oil

Soya bean oil (crude/refined)

Soya bean cake

Copra oil

Castor oil

Maize oil

Groundnut oil (crude and refined)

Sunflower seed oil (crude and refined)

Cotton seed oil

Cotton seed cake

NON ALCOHOLIC BEVERAGES AND TOBACCO

Tea

Tobacco and tobacco manufactures

Coca-cola, Fanta, Seven-Up etc

Malt drinks

Lucozade

ALCOHOLIC BEVERAGES, WINES AND SPIRITS

Palm wine

Kola nut wine

Gins

Coconut liquor

Whiskies

Brandy

Tonic wines

Stouts

Lager beers

ROOFING SHEETS AND OTHER BUOLDING MATERIALS

Corrugated asbestos

Cement sheet

Long span roofing sheets

Building wires

Clear sheet glass

WOOD AND WOOD PRODUCTS

Wood furniture and components

Briquette (charcoal)

Veneer ceilings

Wood charcoal

Wooden designs

Railway sleepers

Bamboo furniture and components

Rattan woven J31. UI dry baskets

Wooden doors and frames

Wall and ceiling tiles

Window frames

Cane furniture

SWEETS AND CONFECTIONERIES

Malta sweet

Tom Tom

Chewing gum

Biscuits

ELECTRICALS/ELECTRONICS

Room Air conditioners

Lamp and lighting fittings

Electric bulbs

Refrigerators

Stabilizers

Welding machines

Battery chargers

Electrical cables

Empty cassettes

Television sets

PROCESSED FOOD ITEMS

Sardine and herrings in tomato sauce

Tomato puree

Tomato paste

Tomato ketch-up

Tropical fruit juice

Spring water (bottled)

Custard powder

Corn flakes

Sea foods, shrimps, lobsters

Adeyemo Aderonke

Honey

Poundo yam (yam Flour)

Soya beans meal

Food ingredients and spices

Copra cake

Fish meal

Linseed cake

Meat/bone meal

Sunflower seed meal

Citrus pulp pellets

Tapioca

Grounded ginger

Grounded melon

Grounded pepper

COSMETICS AND TOILETRIES

Hair products

Shampoo

Body lotions/creams

Soaps and detergents

Perfumes

Toilet soaps

Medical soaps

Sanitary pads

Toiletries tissues

PHARMACEUTICAL AND MEDICAL SUPPLIES

Drugs

Syringes

Hospital beds and beddings

Surgical instruments

GLASS PRODUCTS

Bottles

Mugs

Plates & household products

Windscreen

TELECOMMUNICATION CABLES

100m of A 2Y (A) 2YT (30 x 2 x 0.65m) per km

2000m of A – 2Y

2YT (100 x 2 x 06.65mm)/km

INDUSTRIAL TOOLS AND EQUIPMENT

Process machines

Crushers

Coupling boxes

Industrial machines

Industrial plants for ice cream & paper making

Nylon sealing machines

Milling plants

Basic oil extraction plants

Soap, paint manufacturing plants

OTHER MANUFACTUIRED PRODUCTS

Chalk

Aluminum plates

Candles

Sinks

Wash basins

Bath tubs and other sanitary fixtures

Tooth brushes

Ceramics

Traditional mats

Hand woven garments

Natural spring waters

Water pumps (manual)

SOLID MINERALS

METALIC AND IRON ORES

Aluminum

Iron ore

Manganese

Magnesium

Lead and lead concentrates

Silver

Zinc

Columbium ores

Copper

Silica

NON METALIC ORES

Kaolin

Asbestos

Graphite

Mica

Sulphur

Banixite

Barytes

Magnesite

Anlydrite

Gypsum

Marble

Calcite

Potash

Granite

Colemanite

Silica sand

Potash

Bentomitic clay

Bally clay

Potassium

Feldspar

Tale

Dolomite

Bitumen

Carbon black

Coal

Lime

Surpentine

PRECIOUS AND SEMI – PRECIOUS STONES

Gold

Agate sapphire (different colours)

Kunzite

Topaz

Citrine

Emerald

Golden Beryl

Aquamarine

Goshenite

Zircon

Morganite

Tourmaline (different colours)

Quartz

Ruby

Amethyst

Garnet (various types)

Almandine

Beryl

Pearls

Paintings

Bamboo products

Beads works

African talking drums

ARTS AND HANDICRAFTS

Calabash carvings

Pottery

Hand woven clothes

Hand woven rugs

Hand woven mats

Coconut carvings

Metal works

Cane works

Bronze works

Ivory carvings

Basketry

Ceramic works

Leather works

EXPORTABLE SERVICES

Engineering

Banking

Insurance

Consultancy

Shipping

Cultural troupes

Hotel

Hair cut

Tourism

Law

Information & Communication Technology

Home video, music and films

EXPORT PROHIBITION LIST

Timber (rough or sawn)

Raw hides and skins (including wet blue and all unfinished leather)

Scrap metals

Unprocessed rubber latex and lumps

Artifacts and Antiquities

Wild life animals classified as endangered species and products thereof.

EXPORT FINANCING

Finance is the very essence of export business. Its benefits include;

Meeting working capital requirements

Facilitates assets acquisition

Accelerates economic and national development

Encourages international trade and business expansion

Encourages innovations and creativity

Ease of doing business

Ensures liquidity, profitability and growth

Export financing is very vital for the promotion and development of non-oil export. Exporters are to identify the sources and types of financing available so as to be able to carry out export trade successfully

Nexim Bank: In Dec 2017, the Nigeria export – import bank (Nexim) has invited export – oriented small and medium entrepreneurs **(SMES)** to access the 500 billion export stimulation facility and the 50 billion export development fund to boost their businesses, create jobs, and contribute to the foreign exchange revenue earning of the country. The facilities were made available to Nexim bank last Dec (2017) by the Central bank of Nigeria **(CBN)** for lending at a maximum of 9 percent interest rate.

The improved export financing for non-oil exporters

is to enable them to upscale and expand their businesses and improve their competitiveness.

Microfinance Banks: Some Microfinance can help export promotion and diversification, if effective structures to finance and assist small scale enterprise are established.

Venture Capital: A type of private equity capital typically provided to early-stage high potential, growth companies in the interest of generating a return through an eventual realization such as trade sale of the company.

Pre-Shipment financing: This is a financing arrangement preparatory to shipment which is usually short term in nature.

Post-Shipment financing: Short term in nature and essentially for the period after shipment

Suppliers Credit

Commercial Banks

Crowd funding: whereby people come together and pool resources by contributing towards export trade.

Adeyemo Aderonke

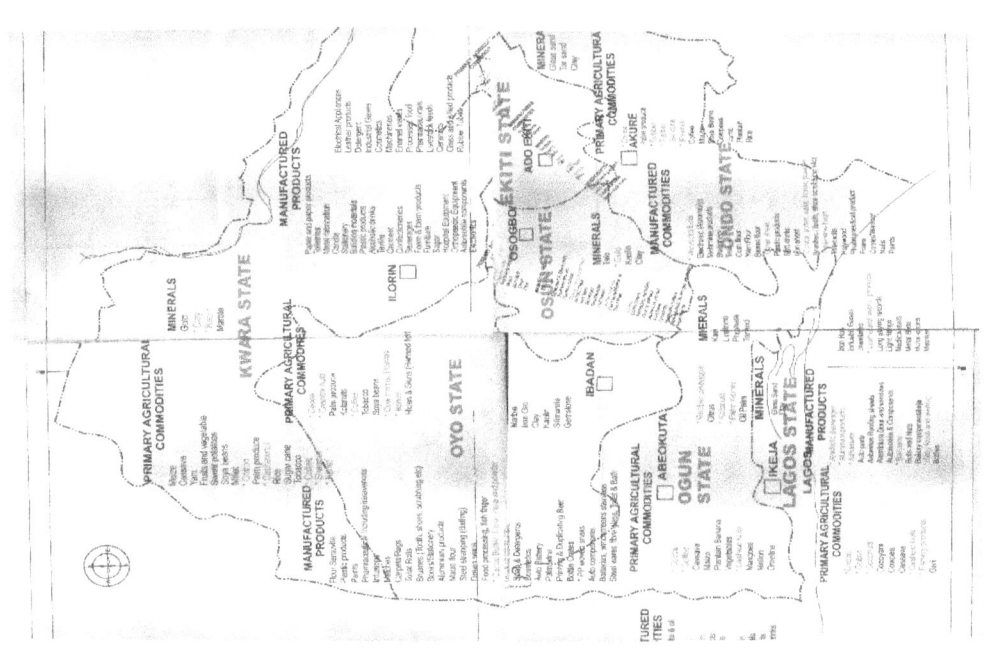

Other books from the same author

1. Parable of the Two Sleeping Women

2. The Beauty of Worship

3. Export Made Easy

ABOUT THE AUTHOR

Adeyemo Ronke runs a faith based ministry known as Sycamore Tree Evangelical Ministry (STEM). She is an ardent soul winner who preaches in prisons, hospital, churches among others. She has a National Certificate in Education at the College of Education in Oyo, Oyo State in the year 1992.

Some years after, she proceeded to the prestigious University of Benin where she studied Literature-in-English and Education. Apart from her academic qualifications, Adeyemo has also acquired professional qualifications which includes a certificate in Aspiring Entrepreneurs Programme from FATE Foundation in 2009.

She is an alumnus of Enterprise Development Centre, an arm of Pan Atlantic University. Adeyemo Esther Aderonke is married with four children.

www.ingramcontent.com/pod-product-compliance
Lightning Source LLC
Chambersburg PA
CBHW052324220526
45472CB00001B/264